Tough Roots

D1430736

Tough Roots
Jean McCallion

Penumbra Press

To my sturdy Welsh ancestors, Ann and Walter Morgan,
who in 1868 confronted a wilderness in the
District of Muskoka and Parry Sound.

Published by Penumbra Press, 7 Aurora Street, Kapuskasing,
Ontario P5N 1J6, with financial assistance from The Canada
Council and The Ontario Arts Council.

Cover art is after an etching by Jo Manning,
Woodlot V, 1978, 27½ X 21½ inches.

ISBN 0 920806 96 1

Acknowledgements

Many of the poems in this collection have never been published. But recognition should be given to the following for previous publication or broadcast: *Cabbages & Kings*, 6X London, 106.9 FM; *Canadian Author & Bookman*; *Northward Journal*; *South Western Ontario Poetry*, *Tower Poetry*.

Certain Ontarians have given much assistance in the research of the Morgan family. They are Bert Foreman of Nobel, a distant relative; Alan Frost, former Rosseau Postmaster; Betty Glenn, librarian at Port Carling Library; Evelyn Longhurst, daughter of a Windermere pioneer and a local historian; Jean Ruth Morgan, granddaughter of Walter and Ann Morgan, and an aunt of the author.

Grateful thanks to Judith Fitzgerald whose interest in these poems included a careful critical reading of a first draft.

A tribute to a poet-friend Catherine Holgate Bankier who read this final manuscript with hearing ears and seeing eyes, and whose encouragement has always been deeply appreciated.

Table of Contents

Author's Preface

The following poems were prompted by discovering in a Rosseau cemetery the graves of my Welsh great-grandparents, Walter and Ann Morgan, who in 1868 settled on land in the Lake Rosseau area, District of Muskoka and Parry Sound. They were farmers who came from Court Farm, Llanvihangel, Pontymoël, situated in rolling countryside near the town of Abergavenny in Southeast Wales.

This farm exists today as a 'gentleman's' farm, the original farmhouse having been built in the thirteenth century. An Anglican church of the same vintage stands nearby, and an ancient inn called *The Horse and Jockey* is located within a stone's throw. Family stories suggest that Walter in true Welsh fashion frequented both establishments.

It seems that Ann made the decision to come to Canada. Walter agreed, and subsequently Ann set out first with some of their five children including my maternal grandfather Edward, who was six years old. The year was 1866, their destination Etobicoke.

In 1868 the Public Lands Act of 1860 was amended by the Free Grants and Homestead Act to encourage settlement in the more northerly regions of the province. According to this provision, 'locations' of two hundred acres were assigned for five years if certain conditions were met. Two acres had to be cleared; a 'shanty' sixteen by twenty feet had to be erected with occupancy during six months of the year. Furthermore, restrictions concerning pine trees and road allowances were to be strictly maintained.

Anyone who has driven north on Highway 400 knows that although its rugged beauty is striking, Muskoka is not prime farmland by any stretch of the imagination. Nevertheless, the Morgans decided to take up the bone-breaking tasks of felling trees, burning slash, up-rooting stubborn stumps, building roads. With other hardy souls they faced the challenge of creating a homestead in an inhospitable wilderness.

A little book, *The Pioneers and Late Comers* by Violet Jocque, records the 1883 death by drowning of Walter Morgan in what is now called Morgan's Bay. Ann outlived her husband by about ten years.

Apparently the Morgans were hard workers and successful farmers, but like the other pioneers, they suffered many hardships. William, Walter's eldest son, inherited the farm. A story goes that he broke his leg; after splinting and wrapping it in a potato sack, he said he didn't need a doctor and could cure himself. He did, the proof being he healed and he walked.

In 1925 the farm was sold and is now divided into cottage lots for the enjoyment of its later owners.

* * *

'We forget our forebears, and yet in ways we do not recognize we share their predicament.' George Woodcock, Introduction to the *Selected Poems* of Al Purdy

Harsh North

Colour it Granite

My blood grew in the north,
spread out in the branches of a tree,
roots reaching rocks scored
by a northern glacier.

Bones of my bones
formed the low mounds
on a high hill, bottom
red mud of a lake and a river.

Here for eons
new beginnings,
unseen endings above
and below surfaces ...
      where
     loons and dead logs float
     on the lake and water lilies
     plunge with their long stems,
     sun on docked leaves,
         jackpines
     claw the sides of cliffs,
     shout to the circling hawks,
     the taloned firs.

  Here
I begin to unwind
   unfold my scrolled story:
    colour it granite.

Glacier Stones

For untold years stones
centred in glaciers
gripped the sides of mountains.

They knew hard passages
perilous rock ledges
ominous arctic air
avalanche to emerging valleys ...

spoke the ancient lore of mountains.

Fierce sagas still thunder
in tossed scrolls of pitted lava:
pressed flowers, wet forest ferns,
tiny animals that twist and turn;

with impress of raindrops
strange footprints in sand

on the edge of this cold northern lake
stones warm as my hands.

To Gather Stones

To gather stones
is to gather me

not in the corner
of a ploughed field –
a statement

not with solemn lines
carve a cairn
upon a rocky headland

not after patient piling up
build a strong wall
or moor a landing.

No! Words in flight
move like Canada geese
above a northern river.

This much and no more
shall stand –
a voice in a stone-filled land.

Northern Autumn Morning

The stars march on
and the drummer moon returns
to his separate quarters.

A lone hawk climbs
to watch the morning sky
gather for manoeuvres.

The sorcerer sun
behind a hill
fans his special fire

strikes a spark upon a rock
ignites an outcrop field
slashes with sharp-toothed shadows
granite.

Not long to wait for
total conflagration of trees
blast of frost in marsh and valley

soldier pines that take the hill
marshalled by wind to face
onslaught of winter.

Tough Roots

Dead as a stone? No.
These roots live.

Quickened by pulsing sun,
a tough tree vibrates outer warmth,

relays inner strength,
feels the tug of stubborn roots.

Unflinching under the lash of storms,
a tree remembers it held fast
when ice catapulted from far north
in lightning hails of thunder.

Isolated in back acres, concrete cities,
stubborn roots stone-contained

resist, no matter what machines
stutter angrily overhead
with great teeth.

Algoma

A land grained in granite,
winds tearing at the throats of canyons,
forests, marshland, wild land,
quicksand and vegetable mould,

where tortuous rivers and creeks
overflow banks, burst into stony lakes
scattering birds and diving ducks,

where ravens shear off tops of
poplars, pines; spiralling hawks
follow trains toiling up
northern shores,
sight their taut prey
swoop to kill.

Circus Performer

Firred North,
majestic and ageless,
you move with a rolling gait

stalk this northern stage
freely on padded moss,
your forests shining.

Under a billowy canopy
circus lovers linger for
your heavy-footed entrance

restless, await your entertainment,
join summer's loud applause,
hot and breathless.

Your pelt grows long and shaggy,
is ruffled by August storms;
bloodshot your lakes
at dawn and sunset.

Believing they can chain you,
men and machines parade your
muscles and your girth, goad you
with their puny drills.

You daunt them with your antics:
compress tremendous strength
into lurching steps
lumber into dance,

high in air toss waterfalls
haloes of sun spray
red-winged birds and dragonflies.

The Oak

In shaking blue air
you stand firm

thick in your skin
incessant spring rain
summer's flood.

Autumn's leaves
do not bruise your roots

frost tonight will not
burrow deep.

Set in your own way
you exceed granite.

Pioneer Family

Deserted Country Church

It doesn't take much
to knock down dust cobwebs
buttressing the porch,

a light push
swings the old door in.

I know we open doors
at our peril

graves too
when tall weeds
command the yard

if one flower
stands on guard –

beards the traveller
at the gate.

Ancestral Grave Found at Rosseau

Ken was the first to see it:
a white blur in dark bushes.

I push aside prickly underbrush
from their fading names,
kneel to scrape scabby yellow lichen:

In
Memory of
Walter Morgan
Departed this Life
July 2nd 1883
Aged
65 years

* * *

In
Memory of
Ann Morgan

* * * * *
* * *

Why do I stand here?
What did I hope to find?

Great-grandparents I never knew,
answers caught in a thicket?

Didn't we come here on a whim and a maybe
(Hey, Mom, let's go for a ride and a swim!)
An escape from summer's heat?
Smooth sailing in Lake Rosseau?

It's too late to offer an oar
to a long-dead ancestor,
comfort a grieving wife
lost between worlds.

Swamped by bobbing questions
in the eyes of my solemn children,
(questions I cannot answer)

I dive in, and save them
the trouble of asking.

Discovery

Ann Jones of Ralston Park

your stone is buried like you
in the soft summer earth
obliterated
                    almost.

I can guess at four lines of
(I think) a poem by H. Boyer
that does great things for you:

begs golden gates to open
at your coming in,

flights of angels
to sing your name.

But no one yet topples trees
piles brushwood
burns slash

builds a structure of strong words
to domicile you.

Foreign pioneer woman –
not a phantom called from
the unconscious, citizen
of another world

you live in my kneeling bones,
in the feel of my fingers probing stone,
tugging at deep-seated roots

in my blood your passion
whirls into motion.

Welsh Settlers' First Sight of Land

With smoke of many bridges clinging
they exchange one wilderness
for another
      the voyage impassive
days piling on days
      until

a mackerel sky splashes the sea
engenders a spray of whitecaps
a whirl of two sporting whales.

Canada West had mapped easily in Wales:
land green, lakes blue, red for railroads,
Montreal and Quebec City black dots.

Theirs for the asking
      an ocean ago
a bush farm now a tossup
an uphill speculation

across a long water
hoot of owls
jawing of a wilderness.

For days calculations
how best to claim a promise
nailed to a coloured poster;

with poke bonnets shading their women's faces
their own caps jaunty on the back of their heads
all eyes search for that first sight of land.

Comes the time of recognition
the hour of revelation –
a smudged horizon:

the Canada West promise
the sole commitment
that fine dotted line.

Cautionary Note

After that uncertain journey
across salt water

sea air fills your lungs
and you enter the St. Lawrence.

When you see the longed-for
shoreline, do not think
you have arrived, have come
at last to a new home.

Far from it – for days
you will be a traveller

your foreign dress
your black silk bonnet
a Welsh sign.

For weeks you will look
about you

catch yourself
in the act of

tying strings
counting children.

Ann's First Winter: Etobicoke

A dead white winter.

I want to pull up
flowers headfirst

prod reluctant roots,
proclaim young shoots

resurrect bare trees,
fasten buds on branches

string my fingers
through green leaves,
relight floral lanterns.

On a robin's dare,
standing in newborn orchards
let wind rearrange my hair –

white clouds fly –
kites in air.

Then I'll bring night down,
carry the moon in my arms
back to a river I once knew –
dream firelight, Wales, you.

Here Where the Wind Turns

Watching the snow
fall
flake
by
flake

I feel the weight of hours
days
months
years of waiting for spring

Here where the wind turns
to blow
light snow
across our valley

here where my bound heart
waits
uptight for unravelling.

Green Isn't Easy

Green is there all right
under last night's snowfall

beside stone fences
in stiffened trees
barely hanging vines
the evergreens.

Who can't remember green
remember buds   leaves
springing branches,
bloom of apple blossom?

Hidden all beneath the surface
movement of other worlds

where no colour disturbs
eyes blinded by sun on snow

and pale moons struggle to rise
early in the late winter afternoons.

Ann's First Spring in Ontario

Spring comes early this year
bearing its ironclad promises

but I do not shout or dance,
celebrations tire me:

> springing grass
> slashed seeds
> sprung bulbs.

Trumpet calls
of straight-back daffodils
    scatter me....

Having abandoned the field,
I wait for
    summer's sallies
    to topple me.

Crocuses

And these crocuses
gathered alongside
houses

not so much
to signal spring
in captive rings

as portent
of hot summer's sting

fierce swelling bees
all swollen things

Trilliums

Spring-coil action
springs earth
wide open

moves mountains
covers stones
colours weather

rock-face and sloping hills
sliding
            into length of rough
days planed down smooth
the sawdust valley;
wet the curled leaves

along banks of streams
white-capped trilliums
slippery trout in green.

Free Grant Deed of Land (1868)

The words read easily:
meaning clear
pages numbered.

It's only at second glance
you notice how thin
paper is.

Ask yourself
if you know
how this land lies?

Where are stony pastures spelled out,
undrained marshes, failed fields,
abandoned lean-to shanties,
tired oxen dragging iron ploughs?

How grows the seed?

How near your next-door neighbours?

Ann's Arrival at Rosseau

Did your quickly exhaled breath
catch on a branch, your words
scatter in winged syllables?

Did muscular flexed rocks
bind the lake
when you saw the rugged shoreline?

When the sun captured you,
galloped you through welcoming skies,
did you fly down to the water

open your arms wide –
gather it all in

say to the hardwoods at the Portage,
the shoving waves crowding the shore,

'I could not ask for more?'

* * *

Did the moon that same night
steal your dreams, carry you
struggling down from clouds

point with a long thin finger
to threatening hills,
fanged forests, unsheathed caves –

lair of wolf and nightmare?

Log Cabin

Ann saw you in Wales,
your label on a bottle
of Quebec maple syrup:

a colonial sun
spun sugar leaves,
woodpecker spiles
tapped trees

uncluttered green
folded smoothly around
a gaggle of geese
white foam

an aproned woman smiled
at your open door;
pines faced windward.

After sugaring-off
    shallow sheetpans
    maple leaf moulds
    lie empty.

Behind your sticky label
    howl of wolves
    bark of foxes

    fields
    overblown with
    seedy promises, back pastures,
    flint, stone, windrow.

Behind a heavy door
    a small-boned
    tight-lipped
    woman.

Fine Oak Pins

'Any fool can find fault, but
it takes a man to do a job.'
          Pioneer Proverb

The beams were straight and true,
squared timber they called it,
each tree seventy to eighty
feet long when felled.

Broad axes had done their work:
logs and split cedar for the roof,
wet moss for cracks,
clean white pine for walls,
flattened balsam for floors,
fine oak pins to fasten.

                * * *

For Ann no shanty now,
no green crotches and poles
covered with brush or elm bark

no beds of green gum boughs
for mattresses, smoothed blocks
for tables, frypan and tea pail
on snags, bacon hanging from a limb.

            Tonight
  by the light of fat pine torches

      Sing! Drink! Be Merry!

      You have raised a roof!

Front Parlour

Family Bibles,
Church of England Prayer Books,
tight Testaments on tables
in front parlours

dust-laden velvet curtains,
slippery mohair furniture,
stuffed owls on glass bookcases,
sideboards with mantel clocks,
oval portraits, pressed glass.

        And
the organ in the corner
waiting primly in its fringed shawl,
stops aching to be pulled,
hymn books closed, sheet-music
curling open

and always
a potted plant on guard in jardinière
a patient fern in the front bay window

listening for approaching footsteps
the weekly Saturday watering.

Ann at Table Saying Grace

Your hands clasped together,
you bow your head,
close your eyes,
say grace.

Behind you
on the cabin wall
a framed Christ
hangs with knitted brow
to bless in brooding wool

the meat
the woven bread
the chosen cup.

Around your hewn pine table
your subdued congregation
waits for feeding.

Ann Watches Walter Chopping Wood

I lean against this tree
tough, sinewed, scaled,
clutching the bedrock
we survive on

soil narrow, sensitive to touch –
this act our bread and butter.

Axe glints in the sun,
wood splits and jumps:

                    I see
fire's hot colour,
feel winter's heat.

            * * *

In Wales I leaned on you,
the two of us rooted in a land
that grew us both, that knew
our shortcomings and goings,
couldn't forgive us your trespasses.

On the strength of a longing
I honed my heart, heard
a northern country
green in whispers, soft shadows,
warm shallows, indulgent shores.

My steady gaze threaded an ocean
and dreamed and dreamed
prophecies with leaves in their beaks,
nests in their heads.

            * * *

Walter, I called to you
across the North Atlantic

you came over dark waters
to clear a bush farm
raise a farmhouse
build a barn.

* * *

Axe glints in the sun,
wood splits and jumps. I see
wood and sawdust fly in all directions
alive and growing ...
all this motion while I stand still.

You pile wood by the fence,
the sun climbs higher and I stand watching.

The day hangs loosely,
no tug-of-war, no pulling apart;
no regret clings like sweat.

Up Country

August and threshing-time:

time to flail
husk from wheat,
forgive trespassers,
forget stubble in fields

in old stone mills
store grain,
turn wheels

in ovens brown with heat
rejoice,
raise loaves,
break bread with friends.

At dusk
milk cows,
light lanterns.

Dance the barn away.

First Thanksgiving After Harvest

That first Thanksgiving the pastor
took bread and blessed it,
broke it, poured red wine
to distribute body and blood.

Never before such feasting:
praising lips
dedicated mouths
divine feeding.

We came
dressed in our Sunday-Go-To-Meeting
best worsted skirts and woven vests

drove patient oxen miles and miles
over miles of planked roads

fields shorn among stumps
where settlers let the fire run

grain long cut and bound into sheaves
stooked capped to cure in the sun

neighbours
travelling through forests of legends
along slippery paths of blazed faith
by streams of living water

together to devour bread
drink wine of vineyards.

Red Against Speckled Green

Red against speckled green
you see it round and steady
promising its special brand

its mixed palette drips....

Reach up greedily
shake it down to earth

cup its smooth ripeness
teeth drowning in longed-for
juices

               Don't

you will be lost among
flowering branches
stirring leaves
rushing senses

               unless you're prepared
for smouldering days
anxious autumns

dark and lonesome nights
snowbound winters

cellars of cobwebbed wine.

Ann Rejoices

Yes, they were red
apples renewed in early glow
of morning light

glossy and firm:
round circle of my heart

done up dark
in bright gingham
under twirling parasols.

Apples sliding on wires
beyond my fingers' reckoning.

Walter Walks Home at Night

The wind comes out of the west,
sky abandons dusk
and you return.

You, Night,
moon compelling
star predictable.

Why do you surprise me?

I know you, have always
known you and your power:

you cancel the sun
make hazardous blazed trails
precipitous rapids.

I walk carefully
in and out of
your white and your black places;
no paved road leads into this bush.

Today I have travelled miles.

When the moon explodes
and the stars ignite

I will return to my love
to my waiting Ann
cabined in your dark –
wrapped under homespun.

Premonition

'Ann hears a tale told at the Monteith Inn'

Beneath topsoil,
sand and weeds,

among dogtooth,
ferns and violets

by the side of an unruly stream
we dug their graves
with our wooden shovels

young river crew
drowning before our screaming
eyes, lungs filling with river water,
heads smashing against piercing stones.

We wrapped them in woollen blankets
three dashing young raftsmen
who had poled wilder rapids

wound them up tight
against the long night.

No granite monuments
no forged iron crosses
mark their scooped graves:

we blessed three cedar slabs
carved with their names

set their water-soaked boots
corked at their feet ...

afterwards left
the three of them.

Walter Drowns in Morgan's Bay (July 2, 1883)

Ann Jones of Ralston Park
I see you watching from a window
for Walter alone in his rowboat;

swirling waters beckon
reach out for him
pull him out of sight;
overhanging branches swim in the bay.

At first he treads laughter,
then flounders, tries to grab
a floating oar –
flails about ... calls out....

* * *

Something washed up on the shore
at Rosseau Falls across the lake
at Stormy Point near Muchenbaker's sawmill

and they called for a basket to put
it trailing mud up from the bottom

in foaming bay waters
sweat sliding
strands of hair swimming
fins floating ... leaves....

* * *

Ann Jones of Ralston Park
I see you standing alone
watching from a window for Walter

a hand shades your eyes.

What it is

You
in my eye
morning
noon
night.

Dusk.

Branches
shine
like shed blood.

In a corner
out of sight
a sliver
of moon.

Night River

Slow flowing river
dark
forbidding

pine trees black
unresponsive
alien.

Two birds flutter
against the sky

fall out of sight
to a sightless eye.

Wet, wet my lashes,
haunted my heart

I travel night rivers
in rudderless dark.

From My Window

Lacklustre slack
the branches of this
apple tree

whose stagestruck leaves
exploded myths

whose star-like blossoms
flocked to summer openings

detached the leaves
dried up the apples
hanging by threads
to jerk in a comic tempo

I alone remembering past
performances

the drama
of parted
red velvet curtains.

I Saw Gold Leaves

I saw gold leaves
  come
       floating
             down

fill with gold
     the cold hard ground

gold leaf-rocking
  through
       the
           air

your absent hand

my vacant stare.

Ann Sees a Shower of Meteors

Walter, the time they told me
you had drowned in the bay
trees crowded down to the shore
rocks stood aside for me to pass.

White-faced the pines that night
with lights of urgent lanterns
men calling to one another
men probing with poles.

I shivered in shadows, wept
your immersion in unholy water

grieved for you black and blue
hanging man a blur set in amber.

Walter, tonight I see
lights of the village try
to steady themselves
in wavering water.

I am calm in the sky's half-light.

Above patrolling pines atop the hill
a capsized boat of shooting stars ...

one split second to blaze as day;
then stars eclipse like bones.

Tonight Read Me in Stones

Tonight read me in stones –
solitary in a wayward field

secure in their lying down,
unmoved by the moon
or rage of hurrying waters.

Tonight read me in stones
not worn down by a river's
surging erosion
               but
restrained under stars,
green flicker of Northern Lights,
teasing of fickle shadows –

stones far from the mad dash
the sting and the splash
flung down by a frivolous ocean.

Homesteader

No spring?

do not fear the barren ground
where no bud breaks a wall
and no branch bends.

An autumn sun shines at noon
whose purple shadows
clothe a late-yield grain

enrich a stubble field
where barns are filled.

No spring?

you are your own good season.

Annual Visit

Upon this burial hill
shape of a hairy clenched fist,
coarse brown grass;

sprawling ungraceful weeds
turn cartwheels,
roots straggle.

Once I bent, pruned, altered.

Today I stand unconvinced,
eye the overgrown mass;
how long will it last?

I grow stubborn as grass.

Does it all end here
in this field of carved streets,
these clumps of tufted cedars

that house of ancestors closed up
below ground level, the stone key
colour of granite?

All gone,
gone underground.

I shouldn't wonder
no one greets me at the door.

I intrude; knocked
many times before, know
I knock at my own front door.

Beat, heart,
beat in your living rhythm!
Lift up in air!

The stones sing in the coloured streams.
The pines clap their hands on the hills.

Wedged In

Absolute as quicksand
straight as a well
secret as swallowing

the will to
knows no maybe
shouts a more definite
yes than dripping water.

Look at each of us
digging our nails in
with that omnipresent
shining dust on our set faces

faster and faster and faster
our fast-beating hearts pumping
fast, never   never   never
never giving out

our teeth gritty with grinding
tantalizing   marvellous
annoying   dumbfounding
sand in our mouths.

Someone Lived Here

'A difficult journey
with many turnings,' she said,
'there at the high point over there.'

And they stopped beside a lake,
cut their trekking short
on a ridge of granite to carve
a home in the shape of a shanty –
twenty by sixteen feet, poles for the roof,
moss, gum clay for the spaces.

        * * *

When field stones whisper in corners
and balsam firs talk in undisguised accents,
in the evening you can see them

men who strode through studded pastures, men
determined to enter thick stands of timber,
saws easy across broad shoulders

spring and summer buzzing on the back of blue bottles;
autumn waiting around corners for hayrides;
winter dreaming of red-eyed hearths.

Women met them who swept earthen floors
bone clean with corn brooms, shook rag rugs –
soups steaming in kettles on cranes swung over open fires.

Picked apples, currants, grapes, wild berries,
hop vines for yeast, ploughed fields, dragged harrows,
sent children to one-room school houses.

        * * *

Always the land, the mammoth land
with thunder of granite, green lightning of zigzag
forests older than Norse sagas, Indian legends.

Not so, shanties, houses, barns,
hastily dug graves,
early morning mist in vacant places.

Not one dint
in this flinty land
to show someone lived here.

Kinship

No Small Matter

Ann, it was no small matter
to gather tearful children,
pack simple belongings,
go down to a ship
in a bristling harbour
       leaving husband in Wales
       on the land
       your forefathers worked ...
and the terror of what has been lost
starkly mapped
on small upturning faces ...

       for a handful of dreams
       a deed of land
       a Lake Rosseau bush farm.

       No small matter to set off alone
on the dangerous sea, dragging
your children dangling like weeds.

At Quebec

I search for you
but your face disappears
among faces of passengers
at the ship's rail.

Ann,
I call out to you,
but you hurry by me
down the gangplank.

The stage for Ontario waits,
horses paw the muddy ground;
when will your eyes
and mine ever meet?

You have settled
back in the dark
of a closed coach
that whirls past me.

The Geography of Grammar

I sit quietly
seeking the right words:
some proper alphabet.

A soundless barrier
between us confounds me
an insurmountable wall
I try to climb over.

I cannot (for breathing too hard,
for not listening to silence).

I am out on a ledge
in another world,
lost in a muffled mist

where my fumbling fingers find
no articulate crevice,
no plausible voice
to keep me from slipping.

What Would We Say?

If you and I, Ann,
sat down together,
what would we say, talk about?

A bush farm?
A sadness?

Talk leaving Wales
and a home; talk
five children and one
foot before the foreign other?

Or weather?
How winter pulls down hardpacked,
makes impossible roads passable;
and summer's black flies, mosquitoes?

Speak the price of salt, flour, pork,
sugar, tea, and a tin of molasses,
coffee and a little spice?

What did you do, where did you go,
a woman in a bush shanty at the Portage?

When rivers and lakes bled with bass,
pickerel and rainbow trout,
did you take down your fishing rod,
pack your gear to hunt rabbit, partridge,
beaver, deer?

And the children? How they would run,
jump, swim and slide until one
of their playmates up and died?

* * *

We sip exotic cups of black Ceylon tea
in the spill of light from a sputtering candle.

You talk about Edward,
Ted, my grandfather, your youngest;
tell me what he was like:
smart at school, knew the Golden Rule;
gave you no bother, good to his mother;
in a wooden pail daily drew water.

At your scrubbed pine table
we speak or stare, grasp
slippery moments, sitting there.

The Glass Curtains Need Washing

I washed them six months ago.

How grey again –
as grey as today
this dull April morning.

Ann, I try to place you
in the foreground
of your northern home
with the sun at the right angle,

but you hang back
shift in shadows.

The curtains shudder in air;
I notice dust on top of the dresser.

When will I vacuum this rug,
polish this floor?

When will you
come out of the shade
into focus,

you and the sun
stand still?

Double Exposure

Ann,
I dial an unlisted number ...
no answer.

Your voice is lost
somewhere in the ether ...

no dials for me to twist and turn
twist and turn   no buttons

snap your image
on my projected screen.

> They tell me
> Ted's daughter
> my mother
> was your living image.

> I never knew her: never
> got beyond the seldom smile
> the roundness of her Welsh face –
> a perfect circle.

> Days telescope into
> daze. I picture her
> upright, ironing
> in a Toronto kitchen:

> after school
> her raised blue eyes
> a quick affirmative nod;

> I snatch a macintosh apple
> from the basket in the attic.

> My legs run.

Ann Speaks

You've had your say;
now it's my turn.

My inner eye
studies maps,
sizes obstacles,
at a glance
levels trees
splits boulders.

I ponder dreams.

Can you catch them
grasp them?

Now and future
woman,

never think
to snatch my hand ...
yank me through
your camera lens
... to find
my steady features
in your snapshots.

Great-granddaughter,
no easy click
will summon me
to your glossy dreams.

Pioneer Courage

What's the difference?

A daughter's first jump

    at 3000 feet

... Nancy   soaring ...

above the Alberta foothills
decked in feathered gear

propelled from a slanted
plane into air

that sucks her lungs

whistles her ears

    drops her

onto a floorless wind

f   l   o   a   t
              d   o   w   n

bump bump bump bump

to dig a rancher's unfamiliar
field trailing a white cloud
not unlike a wedding train?

        * * *

OR

Up and over the sea-road, sleepless
getting the hang of pitching days,
the hold of creaking nights

finding sea-legs on a sloping deck
north winds fierce enough to stop breath,
fray sabre-toothed rigging.

What for?

All for the same things:
      that soft landing
            that safe return
                  those mountains.

Nancy's Leave-Taking

The U-Haul waits.

Soon Nancy starts
her miles-long trek
away from us, drives

down our driveway
left turn to Sterling
across King at the light

to Main, left again,
right to the 403 East Exit
on to Toronto and the 400 North.

... Ann, your disembodied voice
floats like Nan's out a window
of a fast-travelling car....

From the safety of Nancy's eyes
you wave to us – goodbye ...
goodbye ... goodbye....

Kinship

I walk a Muskoka road,
maples, birches, beeches
clamour and chatter.

Ann, you hang back
silent in the cool woods,
wet and green mossy places,

boots muddy, in nineteenth century
head-to-heel muslin, poke bonnet.

You peek out at me with an air of
appraisal, puzzled hostility;

you move,
and I will you to turn and speak
but your shadow follows you

steps over a stile
strides through the yellowing field
keeps up until you pause

shade your eyes with one hand
turn and wave,
for a foolish moment
I think, at me;

        then
I notice you're carrying something
a swinging basket? a lunch pail
for Walter and William?

I look at my watch.

Where has the time gone?

Sunlight Seen Through Glass Curtains

Laced with green leaves,
the glass curtains motionless,
not the glass
for the sun breaks through

and I enter from another room,
pause at the door
to gaze and hesitate ...

for a moment have the crazy notion
that like you, I'll handle
anything that comes
without breaking –

and if all else fails,
with no effort at all
I can pull down a green shade.

Dust in Corners

After long trying
the time comes
when you know
you have to let go
forget dust in corners

leave things
where they lie
stroll far fields
a dog at your side
and a walking stick.

Nothing is owned
everything leased

roots torn up
branches broken
garden gone where
stones now grow.

Paper Cutout of Ann

You are gone
you were never here

merely a thought
for me to hold
between thin leaves
of wood and water.

I look down at my hands:
study their flesh and patterns

fingers,
bones of your bones,
cutting strong and weak syllables

rounding off words of farewell
with this skeletal pencil.

A Place Last Summer

Because you may not find
this place again

this heart-high gate
this leafy tree
the yielding grass

forget
fast-beating wings
and such.

But wandering down
a country lane

kicking stones

disturbing dust

enter

if you must.